Keys To Success

For Kids

Caleb Maddix

Keys To Success For Kids

By: Caleb Maddix

Edited by: Amy Kochek

Cover design: Caleb Maddix

Table of Contents

CHAPTER 1

Excuses Don't Excuse You

O ne afternoon while attending school, I had some free time to read an assigned book, but my mind went away from the book into another world. Then suddenly, my mind came back to the classroom and I began to hear one person saying, "I can't" while another said, "I don't want to." The final sentence I heard was, "It is too hard." I realized the students were complaining, but I didn't allow the complaints to stay in my mind. I was so used to hearing these words that I didn't let it effect me.

A couple hours later in Physical Education (P.E.) class, the memory of those words in the earlier class came to my mind again when my gym teacher assigned laps to everyone based on their behavior during the beginning of class. He went through the names, and my friends all had 1 lap.

When I finally heard my name called, my coach said, "Caleb Maddix, three laps."

Out of shock I screamed, "WHAT!" I was in disbelief that all my friends had only one lap when they were acting exactly the same as I was. Can you believe that? That was so unfair!

"That is all the names, go run your laps," said my coach.

As I ran my laps, I found myself saying under my breath words just as bad as the ones I had heard earlier in the day in the other class. This time I heard myself say, "This isn't fair," and "they talked just as much as I did."

All of a sudden, I remembered something I had heard when I was watching Tony Robbins discussing some keys to success on YouTube. In the video, he emphasized, "no one determines the quality of your life but you."

I realized that this applied here. I deserved the 3 laps, and even though I thought my friends deserved 3 as well, their assignments had nothing to do with my attitude. Even if my friends did run 3 laps, I would still have to run the same amount of laps, in the same amount of time, at the same place. My attitude automatically changed. I realized I was making excuses. Yes, my friends deserved laps, and yes, their smaller assignments might have been "unfair," but I really did deserve the laps I got. I decided to change my attitude.

This does not mean that if something unfair happens to you, you have magic fairy dust (AKA magic fair dust – LOL) to make it fair. But you can always change something, and that something is your *attitude* toward the situation. There is never a good excuse for failure to succeed or failure to be happy. Someone once said, "Life is 10% what happens to you and 90% how you respond to it." When something happens that doesn't go your way, find a way to keep a positive and enthusiastic attitude. Your words are so powerful in any given situation that they have the ability to change the way you feel and act.

The 3 R's

I want to give you guys something that my dad always made me do growing up to help me get rid of excuses, and I still use it now.

It's called the 3 R's: **recognize, refresh, and react**.

Recognize

The first thing that you do whenever you find yourself in a situation that you don't like is to recognize it. For instance, you may recognize that your friend is mad at you because you called him a bad name.

Refresh

The second thing that you do is to sit down and accept responsibility for your part in the situation. You refresh by going up to your friend and apologizing for calling him the bad name.

React

The last thing that you do is to react, which means that you make a decision to not call your friend a bad name in the future. When you react, you are making changes in your behavior so that you don't keep making the same mistakes over and over again. I learned this when I was 7, and I have used it throughout my school years. It helped in so many situations, and I know it will be a huge help for you.

Take this Science class scenario, for example:

You are in Science class and your teacher tells the class not to talk during the assignment. One minute later, your friend asks you for help on problem #4. You help him, and your teacher hears you explaining how to do the problem. She reminds you that you were told not to talk, and she punishes you for not following directions. You get mad and say, "That is not fair. I was helping him." Suddenly, you realize you just made an excuse for your behavior. Your first reaction this time should be to apologize to your teacher as soon as you recognize that you tried to excuse your behavior. Then, think about your three R's:

Recognize

Recognize that this situation is your fault because your teacher told you not to talk. Instead of following directions, you talked to your neighbor.

Refresh

Refresh the situation by apologizing to your teacher and tell her that you will make better choices in the future. Accept the punishment that is given without excuses.

React

React to this situation by thinking about how you will act in the future. From this point forward, you will make it a point to follow directions exactly as your teacher gives them so that you will not get in trouble again.

Reflecting on the 3 R's will teach you to recognize and eventually eliminate your excuses in your journey to the successful life you desire. Always be willing to grow and learn. When you hear excuses come out of your mouth, tell yourself, "Excuses do not excuse me!"

I've done a lot of studying about excuses because I know this was a big area that I wanted to make better. I want to share something else with you because I think this information will help you with the 3 R's as well. One book I read that was a huge help was, The Success Principles, by Jack Canfield. In it, there was a formula for taking responsibility called E+R=O.

E stands for Event, R stands for Response and O stands for Outcome. In most situations, people believe that it is the outcome that makes them live the way they do. When something happens to them, they only focus on the outcome. For instance, if someone lost their leg, they may make excuses as to why they can't be successful, but a girl named Amy Purdy shows why this is not true.

Amy Purdy lost both of her legs because of a sickness that she had. The doctors only gave her a 2% chance to live. After losing her legs, she could have been sad based on her outcome. In fact, many people who have lost their legs pout over their outcome and live their lives in a wheelchair without trying to make a difference or changing their response to the event. Amy took action and chose to respond in the right way to her event. She spent countless hours training to become a snowboarder with two prosthetic legs.

It wasn't easy, but she started competing in snowboarding competitions and won many awards. After that, she became a model and actress and started her own business to help people like herself who had disabilities. She even appeared on the show, *Dancing with the Stars*. Amy used the formula for taking responsibility and found success because of it. The event was that she lost her legs. Her response was to use her disability in a positive way. Her outcome was that she became a successful snowboarder, actress, author, and world changer.

For many of you, the event may be that your teacher gives you a bad grade that you don't deserve. Your response should not be to whine or complain, but you should accept the grade, tell your teacher that you respect her decision, and ask what you can do to improve in the future. The outcome is that your teacher will view you differently, you will learn something new, and you will get better grades in the future.

Are you a Bully?

As I said earlier, words can have a huge effect on your behavior. Many times, when we make excuses, we use negative words that can actually be a form of bullying. In the same way that you can bully other people, you can also bully yourself with the words you speak about yourself. Now you may not think you're a bully, but believe it or not, you can bully yourself by saying words like:

- "I can't!"

- "It is impossible!"

- "I am bad at it!"

- "I am a failure!"

- "I am stupid!"

- "I am fat/ugly!"

- "Nobody likes me!"

If you want to try an exercise to change your mindset and excuse making, perhaps you can follow my example. I was reading this story about Bill Gates one day, and he said that he wanted to completely change the way he thought about himself. He went to the dictionary and looked under the C's. He pointed his finger at the top of the page and moved it down until he found the word, "CAN'T." He took his other hand, grabbed a pair of scissors, and cut the word out of the dictionary. He said he did this because in his world, he didn't even want this word to be in his vocabulary or mental dictionary.

After reading that story, I was motivated to do the same thing. Because I was laser-focused on getting rid of this word from my vocabulary, I bought a dictionary and a pair of scissors and physically cut the word, "CAN'T" out of my dictionary just like Bill Gates. That simple action changed my life. I want you to visualize this and mentally cut out this word from your mind. It will change the way you think and talk about yourself, and it will help you stop making excuses. Instead of being your own personal bully, you will become your own personal encourager.

The words mentioned above are powerful and hurtful. Get rid of these excuses as soon as possible. Once you remove these negative words from your life, you can surely succeed.

Take the Wright brothers, for example! We all know who they are, right? You know, the brothers from Ohio who are known for creating the first successful airplane? The brothers had people left and right telling them, "You CAN'T fly a plane!" and "Flying is for birds, not humans!" and "Humans CAN'T fly!" Orville and Wilbur Wright could have easily felt defeated and given up. Instead, they pushed through that boundary.

They didn't sit around making excuses as to why they couldn't reach their goal. The word, "CAN'T" did not exist in their vocabulary. Instead of saying, "I CAN'T" they said, "I CAN." Rather than making excuses, the brothers made it happen. The Wright brothers' perseverance led them to prove all of their haters wrong! In developing the first successful airplane in Kitty Hawk, North Carolina, Orville and Wilbur Wright soon became national heroes.

CHAPTER 2

Go for the Goal

In the previous chapter, you learned how to stop making excuses and take control of your life, but there is no reason to have control of your life if you do not have goals to help you succeed. Let us define success:

Success: the accomplishment of an aim or a purpose

Whenever I meet a new kid, I always ask him or her this extremely important question, "What do you want to succeed at in life?" Almost 90% of the time, the answer is "I don't know." This response is a sign that this kid has not set any goals. I could not imagine my life without a goal. It would be like floating in space with no purpose or plan.

You Can't Score a Goal Without a Target:

Imagine watching a soccer game and there are no goals at either end of the field. The players get on the field and kick the ball around for an hour. They do some pretty cool tricks with the ball, but without a goal, the game gets old really fast. A game without goals would be really boring, right? I'm sure most of you would have stopped watching after 15 minutes. Why? Because the point of soccer is to get goals. That is what makes it so interesting to watch, and it is also what gets us excited. Fans would not be rooting for their team if there were no goals.

The same can be said about your life. Without goals, your life will be just as boring as that soccer game. You may do some pretty cool stuff with your life, but without a goal, the thrill will not last long. At the same time, you will miss other people supporting and rooting for you because they won't know what winning looks like without showing them your goals.

When reading this, you may find yourself asking, "Caleb, why is it important for everyone in the world to know what his or her goal is?" The reason for this is that if you go through life without a dream or something to accomplish, one day you are going to be working at a gas station telling people the price for the peanuts they are buying. In that moment, you are going to ask yourself, "Do I enjoy waking up in the morning to go to work? Am I happy? Have I made an impact on anyone?" The answer to every one of those questions will be a loud, "NO!"

If you do not know what your goal in life is, what your purpose is, or what you are going to master/succeed at, keep reading to see the 9 keys that I'm going to give you to help you with your goals.

1. Identify/define: what is a *goal*?

2. Make your goal clear

3. Set a date for your goal

4. Write out your goal

5. Keep your goals on display

6. Visualize your goal

7. Tell someone about your goal

8. Make a list of successful people

9. Learn from them

1. What is a goal

Ok, guys let's start by talking about what a goal is. A goal is simply something that you shoot for or something that you want to accomplish.

Example:

I want to own a Ferrari.

2. Make your goal clear

You have to ask yourself specific questions about your goal so that you can get clear.

Example:

If you want a Ferrari, what do you specifically want it to look like? Get so detailed that you are able to write it and draw it out. What color is it? How big is it? What do the tires and rims look like?

3. Set a date for your goal

A goal is only a dream if you don't have a time period that you want to get it done by. This keeps you focused.

Think about how many of your assignments and projects would still be incomplete if they didn't have a due date. Have you ever had an assignment at school with a deadline?

The night before the assignment is due, you feel the pressure of your due date, which motivates you to work hard and focus so that you get it done. You may have to stay up all night, but the fear that you will miss your deadline will give you energy. I can almost guarantee that if there weren't a deadline, you probably wouldn't have finished the assignment.

The same can be true for goals. It is important to have deadlines for your goals so that you remain focused and do what you said you wanted to do. Remember this, your goals are dead without a deadline.

Example:

I want a red Ferrari by December 31, 2017 by 11:00 am.

4. Write out your goal

Writing out your goals is helpful because it keeps them in front of you everyday. It is a daily reminder of what you need to do so that you can achieve your goals. Writing your goals also makes sure that all of your actions that day are based on your goals. You will waste your time if you don't have a clear focus for the day, and goals are a great way to stay focused. Purchase a small notebook or journal and let that be the place where you write down your goals everyday. Write them out at the same time and in the same place every day so it becomes a habit.

Example:

When you wake up in the morning, take out your journal and write down, "I want a red Ferrari by December 31, 2017 by 11:00 am." You write this down when you feel like it and when you don't. It is a reminder that your focus is to do something that will bring you one step closer to getting your Ferrari.

I started writing out my goals when I was seven years old. One of the goals that I had was to be on national television. Each day, I would write it out in my journal along with my other goals. I saw it everyday and made sure that I did something that day to help me reach that goal. Seven years later, I accomplished that goal.

5. Keep your goal on display

Your room should be filled with items that remind you of your goal. This is where you can get really creative. You can use pictures, quotes, drawings, etc. Whatever you would like to use that fits your personality, you can use. Make sure it is something that will immediately excite you about your goal.

Example:

Put a picture of the red Ferrari on your wall. This picture could be one that you drew or found in a magazine. You may also want to decoratively display the date of your deadline. You can even place pictures of other luxury cars in your room as well.

When Derek Jeter was a kid, he used to hang up a Yankee's jersey inside his room because his goal was to play with the Yankees one day. Each morning, he woke up to a visual example of his goal. He accomplished his goal and played baseball for 20 seasons as the starting shortstop for the New York Yankees.

6. Visualize yourself achieving your goal

Before something can become a reality, you have to see yourself accomplishing it first. This is where visualizing your goal comes in. With each goal that you make, you should literally imagine yourself achieving it. How do you feel? What does that moment look and feel like? Who is there? Like a movie, play out the scene in your mind everyday. If you want to be in the NFL, imagine yourself in the football stadium at your first game. Guys, I know this might sound silly, but it really works. You are training your mind to get ready for your success.

Example:

Your visualization for getting your Ferrari may look something like this: You are holding the key in your hand. It is large, silver, and feels cold in your hand. Looking at the red Ferrari parked in front of you causes you to become overwhelmed with emotions. Surrounding you are your parents and other family members. They are cheering you on as you unlock the car and sit in the fresh leather seats.

This visualization can continue based on how much detail you would like to include. The point is that it should create a picture of what that moment will look and feel like.

During a time when Jim Carrey had no money, he wrote out a blank check to himself for 3 million dollars. Each night he would drive out to Hollywood and hold the blank check in his hand. He would close his eyes and visualize himself earning the 3 million dollars. The crazy part is that at the time he had no job and no money, but he visualized himself accomplishing his goal. He did this for years until finally, he got a role in the movie, *Dumb and Dumber*. Guess how much money? That's right, 3 million dollars!

If you want to be successful and achieve your goal, you must do the same thing. You must write it out and visualize yourself achieving it. Let's say that you want to be a singer. You should imagine yourself singing in front of a large crowd. If you want to be a business owner, imagine what it will feel like to earn your first $100. Your imagination is powerful. It can make goal-setting fun, so make sure that you are using your imagination in this process.

7. Tell someone about your goal

Once you have written down your goal and have a clear idea what you want to accomplish, it is now time for you to share your goal with someone else. Make sure that you don't just share your goal with anyone. There will be people that may try to discourage you from achieving your goals or they won't support you. Don't worry about them.

Find someone that will support and encourage you with your goal along the way. Also, they must hold you accountable. That means that they must make sure you are doing what you said you would do so that you can achieve your goal. For instance, the person that holds you accountable should ask you questions about your daily 3 (you will find out more about the daily 3 later on in the book) to make sure that you are doing them. They should also make sure that you don't quit.

Example:

When you pick someone to be your accountability partner, make a list of questions that you want him/her to ask you. For example, "Did you do your daily 3 this week?" "How many actions did you do today for your goal?" "Are you on track to get your Ferrari by December 31, 2017 at 11 am? Why or why not?"

Also, set a time to meet with this person at least once a week. You can do that through phone or online. Either way, make sure that you spend time with your accountability partner at least once a week.

8. Make a list of successful people

With each goal, there will be someone that has already achieved it. That is what is so encouraging about your goal. Someone has already been where you want to go, and they found success.

Example:

Find successful people that own a Ferrari and make a list. Place your list somewhere visible to remind you that your goal has already been accomplished. This will serve as extra motivation. If your goal is to be an NBA player, make a list of the most successful NBA players put it in your journal or on your wall.

9. Learn from them

Not only should you make a list of successful people, you should also study their lives. Most successful people have certain habits or advice that helped them reach their goal.

Example:

The people that you placed on your list did something in their lives that allowed them to earn enough money to purchase a Ferrari. Find out what they did to earn, save, and finally purchase their Ferrari. This will give you extra direction as you try to achieve your own goal of purchasing a Ferrari.

Derek Jeter was one of the people that I studied when I had a goal to become a professional baseball player. I went to baseball games to watch him play, read books about him, and watched his interviews. I memorized his stats and tried to copy his swing and other techniques. I figured since he was successful at what he did, all I had to do was find out what he did, do the same thing, and I would become successful as well. Much of what I learned from Derek Jeter helped me to become the one of the shortest and youngest players on my All Star team.

CHAPTER 3

Score the Goal

I f you want to dream about your goal, take a nap. If you
want to accomplish your goal, wake up.

Believe in *YOUR* goal

It is okay if you don't know what your next step is right
now. It is also okay if you don't know what your goal is.
Most people don't. However, if you are one of those kids who
do not know what your goals are, begin taking the steps
that I just gave you to start figuring them out. Also, you
need to understand that you may not have the same goal as
your parents, friends, teachers, or anyone else. You are
going to have your own personal goals and dreams, so do not
let anyone tell you what they are going to be. Take advice

from people, but goals and dreams have to be something you are passionate about. It is important that you believe in your goals and dreams. Remain confident in them regardless of those who try to talk you out of them.

Set Passionate Goals

As a kid, try to find your passion when you are as young as possible. For example, even though I am young, I knew what my goal and passion were by the time I was seven. Knowing what your passion is will keep you focused even at a young age. Then, when you get out of high school, you won't end up wondering what your next step should be.

Discovering what you are passionate about is not that difficult. Ask yourself questions such as: What do I enjoy doing? What would I do all day without getting paid? What am I good at that other people compliment me on? What can I do for hours, but it feels like I've only been doing it for a few minutes? If you can answer these questions, then you are one step closer to discovering what your passion is. When you know what your passion is, then you can set your goals and have fun while achieving them because you are doing something that you love.

While speaking to college students, Jim Carrey enthusiastically stated, "I have learned that you can fail at doing something you do not love, so you might as well do something you love."

The journey to success should be fun! Make your goal something you love and could do every day of your life. You should be happy when you have to "work" to reach your goal. Your motivation should be your love for the goal and the process of achieving it. When you wake up in the morning, you should not feel bad. It should be the opposite. When you accomplish one of your goals, you should feel excited!

I must warn you. There will be times when you will feel lost and think there is no chance you can accomplish your goal. It is at this point that you will have to work even harder because now you must overcome your own doubt. This is what we call the *grind*. To be honest, the grind is a good sign that you are on the right path to success. Everyone experiences the grind, but the person who keeps grinding will succeed.

Set long and short term goals

You can have as many goals as you want as long as you stay focused on your long-term goal. Your long-term goal is like your big goal and your short-term goal is like your small goal. Perhaps your long-term goal is that you want to attend a certain college. It is okay to also have a short-term goal of getting an A in your high school Math class. In fact, I recommend having other short-term goals.

I actually think it is impossible to achieve a long-term goal without short-term goals. You need to have little goals along the way. If your big goal is to play in the NBA, then you can have small goals like make your high school basketball team, get on the starting line up, and break a school record. Whatever the large goal is, you should have smaller goals along the way.

Setting Big Goals

If your goal doesn't scare you, then it is not big enough. Dream big! Don't have a small goal—make it something that is almost impossible to accomplish. If you set your goal for the moon and fail, at least you will make it to the sky; but if you set your goal for the sky and fail, you will only be a couple feet off the ground. Dream big and don't let anyone tell you that you can't accomplish it.

A successful millionaire named Russell Brunson told one of my favorite stories about setting big goals. During his high school years, he was a wrestler. Because it was one of his passions, he set a goal to make it to the state championship. He was so focused on his goal that by his senior year, he was able to achieve that goal.

Unfortunately, his celebration was cut short when he realized that one of his teammates won the national championship, which was bigger than the state championship. Russell began to think about why his teammate won the nationals while he only won state. It was then that he realized that his goal was to only reach the state championships, so that was what he won. His goal stopped him at state, so he couldn't go to nationals. Russell learned that you never set a goal for the state championship when there is a national championship.

Goals are hard work

You can go through every single step I've written in this book and still not achieve your goals. If you are not doing something every day to achieve your goal, then it will just be words on a paper. It will simply be a wish. It doesn't matter how talented you are. If you do not work hard enough to make your dreams a reality, you will not be successful. Derek Jeter said that hard work beats talent if talent doesn't work hard. You must work hard, and you must grind. One way to start working on your goal is through the daily 3.

The Daily 3

I remember when I first started liking baseball. At first, I really enjoyed watching the games, but then I started getting serious about playing. I had a lot of disadvantages because I was the shortest kid on the team. That meant that I had to work much harder than the other players on the team. My goal was to make it to the All Star Team. In order to do that, my dad made me start doing something called the daily 3.

Each day, I was supposed to do three things that helped me achieve my goal. For me, this included watching a video on YouTube about improving my game, reading a book about how to become better at baseball, and doing my drills. I did this everyday whether I felt like it or not.

If you really want to see your goals become a reality, you need to be doing something everyday to get you closer to your goal. Your daily 3 must be based on whatever your goal is, and you can choose your 3. If you are having a hard time trying to figure out what your daily 3 should be, here is a suggestion:

1. Read 20 min per day – Make sure that this book focuses on your goals. It should be some type of book that shows you how to grow and get better.

2. Exercise 20 min per day – Your exercise should be intentional. It should be more than what you do in your PE class. You should create a specific work out that you do to improve your health.

3. Write the 4 you are grateful for – Be specific about why you are grateful for what the four things you put on your list. So for instance, if you put that you are grateful for your parents, you should say why. "I'm grateful for my parents because . . ."

Once your daily 3 becomes a consistent habit, you can begin to add to your list. We will talk more about this in Chapter 4.

CHAPTER 4

Time Flies But You Are the Pilot

There is a story about a college professor who, while teaching on the importance of planning your time, used a five-gallon jar to show his point. He had fist-size rocks on the desk, and he put them in the jar one by one until he could not fit any more rocks. He asked his class if the jar was full. Since he couldn't fit any more rocks inside the jar, the class answered with a loud, "Yes!!!!" Listening closely to the class he said, "Are you sure?" Then he pulled out a glass of gravel and poured it in the jar.

Next, he poured in a glass of sand and ended by pouring a glass of water over the gravel, rocks, and sand until it was full to the top. All the students were shocked. They couldn't believe how much the professor was able to fit into the jar even after it looked full. The reason he could fit so much in the jar was because he put the big rocks in first.

When it comes to planning your time, the big rocks stand for the important tasks of each day. The gravel, rocks, sand and water all stand for the extra fillers of your day. If the jar was filled with sand and water first, the big rocks would not have fit in the jar. The point of this example is that you had better put your big rocks or your important items in your day before you let the fillers of life fill the jar.

You have to ask yourself what your big rocks are. What are the big rocks that you must get done each day before your fillers start to take over? Remember the daily 3 from the last chapter? These will be your big 3 rocks of the day. If you accomplish these, you will have time for the other stuff that you want to fill your day with. A routine can help make sure that your big rocks are done, and it also can keep track of your fillers as well.

What is a routine?

A routine is something that you do everyday. You probably already have a routine now and you don't even realize it. If you get up for school every morning at the same time, brush your teeth, and eat breakfast, then you already have a routine. A routine will help you with your goal. It creates a list of actions you must do everyday. It also keeps you on track for what you want to accomplish.

A routine is different from a schedule. Many days are crazy, and it can seem impossible for the average American to have a set schedule. Many things change throughout the day. That is why I don't like to teach kids to have a schedule. Although a schedule might be helpful for some, I would much rather teach about how to start a routine.

My routines are simple, but I do them every day. They end up paying off in every area of life. I have routines for different things. I have an overall routine, and then I have a routine for my business. You can have routines throughout the day to help you get stuff done in different areas of your life. For instance, you can have a routine for the morning and after school.

How to set up a personal routine

Routines help you to accomplish the important items in your day before small stuff gets in the way and distracts you. When developing a routine, simply think of the important things you must get done to be successful. Think of what will matter in ten years and then put that in your daily routine. Your daily routine should not include video games or TV but things that really matter.

Don't worry about the small things. You will still find time for the little pebbles like video games or TV. When creating your routine, you need to make it somewhat fun so you will want to do it every day.

Sometimes though, you have to do things you don't want to do in order to help you reach your goal. My routines help me to be healthy, have good relationships with people, grow my business, and develop strength. Your routines need to help you in the areas of your life that are most important.

Make it practical. You have to find a practical routine that you can make happen every day. Sit down, write out a routine, and do not miss a day.

Reward Yourself

It is important that you find little ways to reward yourself for doing your routine so you will want to do it each day. If you do your routine every day for a month, allow yourself to watch TV for an hour or something else that you enjoy doing.

CHAPTER 5

Manners Matter

Some of you may already be rolling your eyes because your parents remind you to mind you manners almost on a daily basis. I don't want to be another person in your life who nags you about your manners, but I do want to tell you that they are important. Showing good manners will cause people to respect and remember you. Here are some examples of good manners that you should use on a daily basis.

- Say, "Please" when you want something. Not only will it be respectful, but people will also become more generous in giving to you.

- Say, "Thank you" when someone does something for you. It makes people feel appreciated.

- Say, "Excuse me" when you bump into someone. Don't give them a dirty look like they did something wrong. Also, when you leave a table or need to interrupt a conversation, remember to excuse yourself.

- Say, "I'm sorry" and be willing to admit when you are wrong. This is not easy to do, but we all make mistakes and should take responsibility for them.

- Say, "Yes Sir" or "Yes Ma'am" when you are speaking with adults. Never answer an adult with, "yeah" or "no."

- Give up your seat if you are somewhere crowded and see an elderly or disabled person, an adult, or (for guys) a female who is standing. A true gentleman would say, "Please take my seat." My dad has always taught me that if they say no, I should stand up and say, "Please, I insist that you take my seat." Even if they don't take the seat, I still feel that a gentleman should remain standing.

- Don't chew with your mouth open because it is disgusting.

- Use your phone when it is an appropriate time. When conversation is going on around you, engage in it instead of texting or playing games. Also, don't use your phone during family times or at the dinner table.

- Open doors for everyone who is behind you. If you open doors for people, who knows what doors they may end up opening for you. Waiting for others to go first is a quality that really stands out to other people.

Manners in Your Communication

Your communication skills are also a way to show good manners. They are the first impression and sometimes the only impression you have on people. You will meet a lot of people in your life, and some of them may be very important. Some of the important people may have a big part in your success and may be able to impact you greatly.

I assure you, if you follow these tips, people will be impressed by how different you are from other kids and will respect you for it. They may even help you succeed. Also, you never know whom you are talking to when you meet a stranger, so you should always respect each and every one of them. Here are some tips to help with your manners when you are communicating with others.

Tip #1: Eye contact

This is the tip my dad stresses to me the most because looking someone in the eye does four things.

1. Shows you care.

2. Shows you respect them.

3. Shows you are listening to them.

4. Shows you have confidence.

When most kids communicate without making eye contact, it can appear that they don't care, respect, listen, or have confidence. If you are a kid that tries to always make eye contact, others will notice that there is something different about you. They will be more willing to help and invest in you if you look them in the eye.

Tip #2: Introducing yourself to people

Introducing yourself is a simple process. First, identify the person you are going to introduce yourself to and ask questions like, "Are they in higher authority than me?" "Are they male or female?" These questions will come in handy later. Then, all you have to do is walk up to them with confidence, look them in the eye, and say, "Hello, I am (insert first and last name)." If you say your first and last name, people are more likely to remember you.

Tip #3: Names

After you have introduced yourself, ask them their name if you don't already know it. Now, this is where the questions that you asked when you first saw them come in handy. If they ended up giving you their first and last name and are an adult, then you call them Mr. or Mrs. _____. If they are younger than you, then call them by their first name. Out of respect to grown-ups, you will want to use a respectful title. Other than knowing when to use Mr./Mrs. or their first name, it is very important to remember the name of the person you are talking to.

There are many techniques that can help you remember names. One of the ways to remember people's names is to imagine throughout the whole conversation that their name is written on their head. It will associate their name with them and when you see them, their name will pop up in your memory.

Another way to remember them is if you have a friend or relative that has the same name as they do, you can imagine you are talking to that friend or relative. If you ever see the person again and you remember their name, they will feel appreciated. Also, try to use their name as much as possible during the conversation. Make comments like, "(insert name), what do you think about this painting?" Use their name before questions often. You do not want to overdo it though. One last tip about names is to use their name before and after a conversation. For instance, "Hello, Lucy. How are you?" Or "See you later, Lucy. It was nice to talk to you."

Tip #4: Handshaking

Once you meet someone, give them a handshake. You should shake their hand right when you tell them your name. The firmness of your handshake is will vary depending on who it is. Here is a little scale.

- Elderly women = Not hard

- Elderly Man = medium

- Women = A little bit above medium

- Man = Firm, but not as hard as you can

Giving a handshake will communicate that you are mature and well-mannered

Tip #5: Volume when speaking

When you communicate with others, speak up so you don't sound timid. On the other hand, don't speak so loud that is sounds like you are screaming. Speak loud enough for the person to hear you clearly.

Tip #6: Body language

What is body language? Body language is communication from the movement or attitude of the body. Basically, it means that you tell people things about yourself by the way you act. My dad told me that you can tell more from body language than from what is coming out of a person's mouth.

You can tell if someone is sad or happy just by how they look. If I told you I was sad right now, what do you think I would look like? More than likely, I would have a straight face while slouching with my head down.

What if I told you I was sad, but I was smiling? You would probably think that I was not really sad. It is all about how we act and look.

If you are having a rough day or you are sad, try to still show positive body language. Always smile, and eventually you will start to be happy. Really, try it sometime! People want to be around someone who smiles and is happy because they will start to feel happy as well. Positive body language and moods are contagious. You can change people's day for the better. In addition, people will say, "Man, he is always happy." Next time you are down, change your body language and attitude, and you will change how you feel.

Give to others

Be a helper

Successful kids should always to be willing to help others. If you truly want to succeed, you must be able to see the needs of others. Any time you get a chance to help, take it. Our overall goal should be to help as much as we can. If we really took a moment to look at our lives, we would realize that we are all privileged. The fact that you are living and breathing right now shows just how privileged you are. Someone always has it worse, and it is up to us to help that person who is perhaps less fortunate. We must have compassionate hearts. Your life will be blessed when you choose to help without expecting anything in return.

Helping is not just feeding the homeless. It may be picking up a water bottle on the ground or helping your friend with a situation in their life. You can always find a way to help

Be an encourager

Each day there are so many messages we hear that say we aren't good enough, we don't have the right clothes and shoes, or we don't look as good as other people. Because of this, there are usually many moments during the day when we can help others feel better about themselves. As leaders, we need to encourage others. Sometimes you can make someone's day just by simply saying something nice.

You never know who needs encouragement, so give it to everyone. People like hanging out with the person who encourages others. The people who encourage are the ones who are different. They are the ones who stand out and the ones who will succeed. One word of encouragement might make someone remember you for a lifetime. Go out of your way to be kind. You will not regret doing it, but you may regret not doing it. Anyone can be negative and tear people down, but successful people know the art of being an encourager.

CHAPTER **6**

Learn

When you hear the word, "learn," many times you may think about sitting at a desk in a classroom with a teacher standing up in front of the room giving you stuff to write on a piece of paper. While there are parts of this type of learning that you need, I want you to get the idea out of your head that the word, "learn" is a bad word. As kids, learning can mean that we are going to have to do hard work. We think that when it's time to learn we have to sit still and listen to something boring that we don't really care about.

There are times when this may be true, but the type of learning that I am talking about should not bring that same emotion. I do want to say first that learning is hard work.

45

However, anything that is worth doing is going to be hard work. Your brain is one of your biggest and most important muscles in your body. Just like every other muscle, you must exercise it in order to keep it healthy and working properly.

Have you ever seen someone with really big muscles? I mean the type of muscles that look like they are about to pop out of a person's skin. I guarantee that the people with those types of muscles work hard in the gym. They probably go the gym everyday and challenge their body by lifting heavy weights. Each day, they try to lift bigger weights so their muscles can grow, and they can become healthier. You wouldn't have to ask them if they had to work hard to get those muscles. You can see their hard work just by looking at them.

The same can be said for people who don't go a day without learning something new. Just like someone who does exercises every day to make their body stronger, successful people do some form of learning each day to give them more information about how to be more successful? Bulging muscles show someone's hard work with exercising and success shows someone's hard work with learning. You don't have to ask a successful person if they are learning, their life shows this to be true.

Here is the best part about learning. When you realize that learning doesn't have to just be done at school and that you can decide what learning looks like for you, you can be creative and actually have fun doing it. I know this sounds crazy, but stick with me for a minute. Learning can be unique and creative based on how you learn best. You may like to listen while others teach or you may like to watch videos. Either way, you must know the way that you learn best and do something everyday to make sure that you are learning something new.

Do you know what you are doing right now? Learning! That's right. You are reading this book, which means that you are hopefully learning something. This brings me to one of the best ways to learn, which is to read. Once again, I know this is probably something that most of you don't do because you think reading is boring.

However, when you are focused on your future and your goals, you will choose books that interest you. That is the key. If you want to be successful, books that give you the steps towards success should excite you. While reading those books, you should be writing notes and studying the information because it is like you are reading a map that is taking towards great success.

Power of a Book

I remember one time when I was at my friend's house and we were hanging out in his room. His mom came in and handed my friend $20 and then walked out of the room. I was completely shocked. I said, "Dude, why did your mom just give you $20." It was then that my friend told me that he got $20 allowance a week for doing chores. I thought this was a genius idea that I had to share with my dad. I loved money and I wanted to earn more of it, so I thought an allowance was a great idea.

When I told my dad about this allowance idea, he didn't like it. He said, "Son, I expect you to do things like take out the trash and clean your room. I'm not going to pay you for what I expect you to do. When you get older, no one is going to pay you to do those things. You will be expected to do it. But, I will pay you for something that you are actually going to get paid for. I'll pay you $20 for every success book that you read."

My dad knew that all of the knowledge that I would get from reading these books was going to help me become more successful. Becoming more successful also meant that I would earn more money. My dad told me that when I got older I would get paid for what I knew, and the more I knew, the more money I would make.

This motivated me to start reading. The first book I read was, The Success Principles, by Jack Canfield. If some of you saw this book, you would probably freak out because it is over 400 pages long. It looked like a textbook when I picked it up. It took me a while to get through it, but I made sure to take notes and pay attention to what I was actually learning.

After I read the book, I wrote a report about it, and my dad gave me $20. I did this same thing after every book I read. All the books that I read motivated me to write my own book at the age of 13. Also, the information I got from those books is what I used in building my business, coaching people, speaking to thousands, and writing my own material.

This is where learning became fun for me. Like I said before, as kids we think that learning has to be boring. That is just not true. Learning becomes fun when you focus on your goals and passion. We spent a lot of time talking about goals and passion in the earlier chapters so at this point, you should have some idea what your goals and passion are. That is a huge step in your success journey.

I knew that I wanted to read success and business books because I wanted to be a successful entrepreneur. This made my learning fun. I also wanted to play major league baseball, so I read books that helped me learn more about baseball. I would get so excited about the information I was learning that I would lose track of time. You aren't going to fall asleep reading a book that is pushing you towards your goals.

Below I'm going to list the top 10 books that I think all kids should read. I have read all of these and have learned so much from them. I also included an eBook that I published, which will help you find balance between being a kid and having success at the same time.

1. Positive Dog, by Jon Gordon

2. The Success Principles for Teens, by Jack Canfield

3. Seven Habits of Highly Effective Teens, Sean Covey

4. Think and Grow Rich, by Napoleon Hill

5. How to Win Friends and Influence People, by Dale Carnegie

6. No Excuses, by Brian Tracy

7. Mind Gym, by Gary Mack

8. The 10x Rule, by Grant Cardone

9. Winning with People, by John Maxwell

10. How to Have Success and Still Keep Your Childhood, by Caleb Maddix

Once you read all 10 of these books, make sure that you connect with me on social media and post your favorite book. Tell me why it was your favorite.

YouTube University

Reading is one of the most important forms of learning that you can do everyday. Another tool that can help you learn is found on your computer or smart phone, and that is YouTube. Our generation is luckier than our parents and grandparents because we literally have access to millions of videos filled with useful information, and it is FREE. That is absolutely mind blowing.

Obviously, with any technology, please make sure that you check with your parents before you get on YouTube. Have a meeting with your parents and explain why you would like to get on the site and the types of videos that you plan on watching. You may even show them some examples of the videos so they get a better idea of what you will be viewing.

If you wanted to learn any song on a piano, you are one search away from getting a one on one lesson. In fact, if you are trying to get in the NBA, how would you feel about having LeBron James as your coach? For those of you that want to be singers, how valuable would it be to receive tips and lessons from Taylor Swift as your singing coach? YouTube makes all of this possible. There are so many videos that you can watch that feature successful people who are already doing what you want to do. You can learn from them by watching their performances, interviews, or reviews.

When I was younger, I wanted to be the shortstop for the New York Yankees. My favorite New York Yankees player at the time was Derek Jeter who then became my personal coach. How? I watched countless videos on YouTube that had him in it.

You can learn anything and talk to anybody on YouTube. The same can be said for the Internet. There are articles and videos that you can watch by simply typing in a key word search into Google. Instead of spending your time on entertainment, make sure that you are using your technology as a tool to help you learn. Remember, your routine should include some form of learning. Don't use your technology just for fun; use it for the big rocks in your day that we talked about earlier.

Get Hungry

The person that is hungriest to learn will always be fed the most results. If you want to know more about your goals and the secrets to success, you will start educating yourself. The key to learning is to keep educating yourself. You can't wait on someone else to motivate you or offer to teach you something. You have to be the one to search for teachers. That is the point of books and the Internet. You are the one that must start searching for the right teachers. Once you find them, become a focused student that is ready to learn every day. It's almost like going to school. Decide that you are going to wake up early, get in a quiet place, focus your mind, and learn.

You cannot really be serious about success if you are unwilling to learn. If you spend most of your day playing video games, watching tv, or playing on your cell phone, then you are wasting valuable time that could be spent on your goals. Don't get me wrong, there is nothing wrong with relaxing and having fun, but that should not take up your entire day. You must spend time each day learning something new. Don't let another day go by without learning more about accomplishing your goal through reading or watching informational videos.

Getting a mentor

Using the Internet and books will prove to be useful on your journey towards success. However, you should also be searching for a mentor that can help you. A mentor is simply someone that you trust to train, teach, and give you advice. Your mentor should be someone who has accomplished more than you and has some knowledge about how you can achieve your goals. I have been able to find some amazing mentors, so I want to share some tips with you for how to find a mentor.

1. Get their attention: Once you find someone that you would like to mentor you, do something to get their attention. More than likely, this person is busy, so you have to be creative. I had a buddy that sent his mentor 50 pizzas to his home with a note that said, "I want you to mentor me. Here is my number." The guy was so

impressed that he decided to invest in my buddy. Getting attention doesn't have to cost you money either. You can simply message them on social media, send them an email, or write them a letter. The goal is just to get their attention.

2. Provide value: A relationship with a mentor will not be successful unless you provide value to them. You have to understand something. The person you are reaching out to may get asked every single week, "Hey, can you mentor me?" That makes you one of the many. The thing that will separate you from the others is providing value to them.

3. Apply what they tell you: Many times a mentor will test you before they decide to invest in you. They may give you a little piece of advice and watch what you do with it. If you don't do anything with their advice, more than likely, they will decide not to mentor you. On the other hand, if you immediately apply everything they tell you, they will want to mentor you.

CHAPTER 7

Earn

Oone day I was doing research and discovered that almost every single billionaire was making money before the age of 20. I found this fact interesting because for as long as I can remember, I have been selling something. My dad told me that when I was 2, I would walk out to the pond and pretend to sell bread to the ducks. This desire to earn started at a young age and followed me into my school years. I loved sales, so I tried to figure out a way to sell something at school.

I started with erasers. I would buy a pack of erasers for less than a dollar. I would then draw on the erasers. This is where I got creative. I started with the Yankees logo because I became really good at drawing it. I realized that there were other people in my class that liked the Yankees as well, so I drew the logo on the eraser and put their name under it. I would then show the eraser to the person and tell them that they should buy it for $10. Amazingly enough, people bought them. I then started asking other people what their favorite team was. I learned to draw the logo, put their name on the eraser, and sold it to them for $10.

After my eraser business was erased away, I decided to try something new. There was a kid in my class who was a really good drawer. I partnered with him to start making money. I would ask other kids questions like, "Do you like drawings?" and they would say, "Yes." Then I would ask, "Do you like yourself?" and they would say, "Yes." Next, I would ask, "Would you want a customized, 3D, cut out drawing of yourself that you could put on your wall?" They would get super excited and be ready to purchase the drawing of themselves. I would then get my artist to draw the picture, charge the person $20 and give some of the money to the artist.

Use What You Have to Earn

You don't have to be an adult to start earning money. You can earn money right now no matter your age. I know kids that have written books, sold bookmarks, baked brownies and even sold their services to other people. Like I said before, everyone has a talent that they can use to help them earn money.

If you are still stumped about how you can make money, I'm going to give you 7 ways to make money as a kid.

1. Lemonade stand

2. Write a book

3. Start a business

4. Mow lawns

5. Selling something door to door

6. Cooking or baking

7. Sell your talent

You can go online right now and find a list of kids that are running successful businesses because they started selling something to their friends and families. Mikaila Ulmer is an 11 year old who started a business selling lemonade.

Eventually, she sold her lemonade to Whole Foods grocery store. Bella Weems started a business called Origami Owl because she liked designing lockets and bracelets. She started selling her jewelry because she wanted to get a car. She is now a millionaire and her jewelry is widely popular. Jeremiah Jones started designing t-shirts when he was just 8 years old. He sells his shirts online and has already made over 1 million dollars. Earning money has never been easier for kids who have a desire to sell something of value to other people.

Work Your Face Off

Earning money can teach you so many lessons, but one of the most important lessons that you will learn is work ethic. Work ethic just means how hard and honestly you work. The list of kids that I put above didn't just magically make money. They also didn't just have an idea. They put work behind their dream and their idea. Every one of you that is reading this book has a gift and talent that no one else can do just like you. The problem is that many of you don't have the work ethic to make this gift and talent make you money. It is hard to be a business owner. It is even harder to be a successful business owner because it requires a lot of work. You will have to stay up late, work the weekends, and say no when everyone else is saying yes.

I remember one time my friends asked me to go fishing with them. I told them that I had to work. They laughed at me and encouraged me to ditch my work so that I could spend the day fishing with them. I actually really wanted to go fishing. Relaxing at the beach always sounds more fun that putting in hard work, but I knew that I had goals that I had to work on. I told them to go without me and I spent the day working.

I must have made 80 sales calls that day and no one was buying. My hands were literally shaking. That's how long I was on the phone. My friend then sent me a picture of him holding a fish while he was on the boat. He texted me and told me to take a break from work and come fish. I was so tired of making calls at that point that I almost agreed. Before I said yes, I decided that I was going to make one more call. The one call I made was a $1,000 sale.

As a business owner, I know that I can't just chill with my friends and play video games all day. I have to put in the work everyday and say no to the good so I can say yes to the best. That is the cost of success. You will have to say no sometimes so that you can put in the hours of hard work that are necessary.

When you have to work for what you want, you treat it differently. That goes for anything you earn. If you have to work for a video game or pair of shoes, you will treat it differently once you get it because you know how hard you had to work to get it. I remember a time when I really wanted to speak at this event. I begged my dad to let me go, but he said that I would have to earn my way there. I had to find a way to get money that would cover travel, plane tickets, and the money my dad would miss out on because he would have to attend the event with me.

After adding up the expenses, I found out I had to make $10,000 in 7 hours. I knew that one of my strengths was using social media to grow a business. I decided to create an online course and sell it for $1,000. Within hours, I sold 10 of those courses, and I hit my goal. This event was one of the most memorable ones that I've attended because I earned my way there.

The point is that if you want to earn money, you will find a way to do it. Once you do, you will treat that money differently because of the hard work you put in. Get creative and know that you will have to work your face off in order to make money doing what you love.

Divide Your Money

After you get money, it is important that you don't just spend it on food or video games. Remember, everything we are doing is supposed to help you get to your big goal. We are building a life for you so that you can be successful. When you earn money, it should be divided. You should save, invest, spend, and give. Saving each time you earn money will cause a small amount of money to grow. This money can be used to make big purchases in the future so don't forget to save some of your money.

When you invest your money, it should be in your business. I know you may be saying, "Caleb, I don't have a business." You may not have an official business, but whatever you are doing that is allowing you to make money can be considered your unofficial business. With that being said, you need to set aside some of your money to invest back into your business. For instance, if you bake brownies and sell them, part of the money you make should go back towards purchasing supplies to make more brownies.

Since you are doing the work to make the money, there should be some set aside for you to spend. Don't go overboard and blow your money on a bunch of junk, but you can use some of your money to buy items that you want such as clothes, video games, or shoes.

This is the most important part of earning money. You should ALWAYS give part of what you earn. How you give is completely up to you, but you need to make sure that you are giving to someone or an organization that is in need. For instance, each time I earn money, I find a homeless person, fatherless child, or single mother to bless. There are so many ways that you can help other people who are in need. My dad and I try to find fatherless kids and buy them a brand new pair of shoes. It sounds like a simple act, but the look on those kids' faces makes me feel better than any amount of money that I earn.

That is really the whole point of earning money. It is not so that you can become richer or get more things. All of your things are going to break or become unimportant. Money is important, but it won't last forever. However, the impact that you leave on another person's life will last forever. We are going to discuss this more in the next chapter, but I want you to remember that the end goal of earning is giving so that you can make a greater impact.

CHAPTER 8

Return

I remember when I was doing an interview and I was asked what I was most passionate about. Without a thought, I said I am most passionate about making an impact. I believe that your desire to make an impact should be bigger than your desire to make money. The greatest way you can impact someone's life is through giving.

You must be a giver. Even though I am young, I have enjoyed some pretty cool moments and met some successful people. I've been able to enjoy a small amount of success and fame. All of this has been a lot of fun. However, my end goal is not to simply be famous or earn a bunch of money. My end goal is to leave an impact, add value to others, and give as much of my time and money as I can to others. I don't just say the words, but I try to live a life of giving. I want to encourage all of you to do the same.

Your goal should not be just to make money so you can get nice cars, a big house, and name brand clothes. While this stuff may come with more money, it should not make you lose focus of those who are less fortunate. There are so many ways that you can give to others.

It doesn't have to just be with your money. Whether you give someone your time, an encouraging word, a smile, or money, you should always seek to change someone's life for the better. Don't let this world change your smile let your smile change the world. Make someone's day better by giving of yourself in some way. I'm going to give you some examples of ways that you can give back, but you can come up with your own as well. Put the same effort into giving that you do into learning and earning. Make it a goal to give back every day.

1. Be Kind

I want everybody reading this book to ask themselves if they have bullied someone, been bullied, or seen someone being bullied. Almost every single person will most likely answer yes to one of those questions. To me, that shows that bullying in the world is getting worse. What you say to others and yourself matters. There is power in what you speak. You constantly hear stories about people shooting themselves because they are tired of hearing insults and being bullied.

You may not realize it, but one mean thing you say might end up making someone hate their life to the point of death. You must understand that what you say is very important, and your words are powerful. The good news is that there is positive power in your words that can give life, so I challenge you to use your tongue to speak life to others.

Just like one word can end up killing someone, one word can also end up changing someone for the good. I realize that we can't completely stop bullying because there will always be someone being unkind. However, I do believe that we can help change people's lives by simply speaking one word of encouragement.

I challenge you to say one kind thing to three people every day. There are some rules though. Every day it has to be a new person. That means if one day you say something nice to your dad, the next day it won't count if you say something nice to your dad again. You can say something nice to him, but you still have to say something nice to three new people.

Giving someone an encouraging word is one of the greatest returns that you can make each day and it doesn't cost you anything. This will also bring you more joy into your life because of all the positive energy you are giving to other people.

2. Help kids who have no father

It has been said 80% of criminals come from fatherless homes. I really don't have to say any more than that. One of my personal passions is to buy a new bike or a nice pair of shoes for fatherless kids. Even if you can't buy them stuff, you can always be a friend to the fatherless and be kind to them. Here are four ways that you can help the fatherless:

- Buy them a new bike.

- Invite them to do something fun with you and your family.

- Buy them a nice new pair of shoes.

- Be a friend to them and include them so they feel like they belong.

3. Serve the homeless

There are 3.5 million homeless in the U.S. alone. You should treat a homeless person the same way you would treat a celebrity. It is very important to show kindness to them and to make them feel like you care. From the time that I was very young, I have gone with my dad to pass out sleeping bags to the homeless late at night and give Starbucks coffee under the bridge at 5 am. I really enjoy and look forward to giving back to the homeless.

4. Be healthy

Childhood obesity is a growing problem in America. Many kids are overweight, and their health is suffering. Unhealthy lifestyles and habits will only get worse as you get older. You cannot pour into someone else's cup if yours is empty. Giving will become more difficult if your poor health becomes a burden in your life. An unhealthy life can damage your body as well as relationships in your life. I want to encourage you to eat healthy, exercise, and get proper sleep. These will help you stay healthy and increase your energy. When you live at this high level of health, it will be easier to give and help others.

5. Volunteer

My dad used to take me to nursing homes to spend some time with the elderly each week. I loved the time that I spent with them because many of them no longer had family that came to visit. There are so many opportunities for you to volunteer your time to help your community. You can even take a walk at a park or local business and pick up the trash. If there is someone in your neighborhood that needs their lawn mowed or their dog walked, volunteer your time to offer them help. Your time is precious, so it is a definite gift for you to give someone your time and effort. Make it a goal to volunteer 1- 2 times per month.

6. Random act of Kindness

Do you have something that you no longer use or wear that you can give away? Does your mom need help cleaning or organizing something? Is your classmate having a rough day and in need of a card or a nice note? If you open your eyes, there are opportunities to be kind each day. When you do something kind without being told, it is a little more special because it shows that you are looking for people to help.

Returning should become a way of life for you. Each day you should wake up with a smile on your face because you know that you are going to make someone's life a little better. When you live for others instead of focusing only on yourself, you will be happier.

CHAPTER 9

The Truth about Failure

I want you to think of success like a gift you receive on Christmas. You can see the shape of it, and you know that inside the wrapping paper and box is a valuable gift. In order to get to the gift though, you have to unwrap it and open the box. There is no other way to get to the gift. The same is true for success. It is indeed a gift, but it is wrapped up in layers.

One of those layers is failure. That might sound so weird because we have been taught that failure is the opposite of success. The truth is that failure is a part of success just like wrapping paper is a part of a gift. It brings you closer to success until it eventually brings the gift of success to you.

There is a truth that I must share with you, and that truth is that success does not come to everyone. The reason for this is that success is not easy. As you are probably learning, it is hard work and will make you stand out from other kids. One of the hardest parts of success is learning that it does not come without failing. I know the word, "fail," sounds bad because we have been taught that if we fail in school, we are not a success. However, I don't believe this. While failure isn't fun and it doesn't always feel good, it is necessary if you are going to be a success.

Don't Fear Failure

There are times when you are going to take risks and still fail. You may even have an idea that you start working on, but it fails. From what others have said about failure, you may see this as a bad thing. Because of this, you may start to become afraid of working on your goals.

Most people are afraid to fail. I think the fear of failure is so unhealthy and the biggest roadblock towards becoming successful. In order to be successful you must be willing to fail. Failure teaches you so many things that you wouldn't have known. For instance, failing a test or assignment makes you go back to your textbook and relearn information that you may have missed. During this time, you may begin to discover facts that you didn't remember the first time you learned them.

Also, if you fail at your goal, it is an opportunity to try again. This time, you know what doesn't work, so you can start working again to find something that does work.

Life is not about how much you fail; it is about what you do after you fail. I cannot name a successful person who has not failed. Just to give you an idea, here is a long list of successful people who have failed.

- Henry Ford, founder of Ford Motor Company, failed five times before achieving success.

- R. H. Macy, founder of Macy's Department Store, had seven failed businesses before succeeding.

- Soichiro Honda, founder of Honda Car Company, was turned down by Toyota and was jobless until he succeeded.

- Bill Gates, CEO of Microsoft and the richest man in the world, dropped out of college and started failing in business until he created Microsoft as we know it.

- Colonel Sanders, founder of KFC, had his chicken recipe rejected 1,009 times before it was accepted.

- Walt Disney, founder of Disney, was fired from his newspaper job because he wasn't creative, and his ideas were considered bad.

- Albert Einstein, perhaps the smartest man ever and Nobel Prize winner, didn't say his first word until he was four years old and couldn't read until he was seven. That caused his parents and teachers to think he was handicapped, slow, and anti-social. He was also expelled from school.

- Thomas Edison, inventor of the light bulb, was told he was too stupid to learn anything. It also took him 1,000 unsuccessful attempts before producing a successful light bulb.

- Oprah Winfrey, richest woman ever and a TV icon, was told she was unfit for television.

- Harrison Ford, starred in many movies including *Star Wars* and *Indiana Jones*, was told by film executives he did not have what it took to be an actor.

- Elvis Presley, famous musician and singer, was fired after one performance, and his manager said, "You ain't going nowhere, son. You ought to go back to driving a truck."

- Michael Jordan, no doubt the greatest basketball player ever, was cut from his high school basketball team.

I could go on forever, but I think you see my point. You should never be afraid to fail. The greatest people in the world fail. Why? Because they take risks, and in order to get what successful people have, you must do what successful people do. Take risks, fail, work harder, and you will eventually succeed. Don't let anyone tell you that failure means you should quit.

Keep working hard even when people tell you that you should quit. Always work harder even if failures come. Wayne Gretzky said it best when he stated, **"You miss one hundred percent of the shots you don't take."** You will never know what's on the other side of failure if you quit. Failure is the sauce that gives success its flavor.

CHAPTER 10

The Power of Application

I saved this chapter for last because it is the most important. You have spent time and effort reading this entire book and you now have come to the end. Hopefully, you have taken some notes and learned a great deal of information. All of that is important, but at the end of the day, without acting upon the information you just read, you just wasted a whole lot of time.

There is a phrase that I use a lot that states, "Information + Application = Transformation." Each chapter of this book gives you specific information about becoming successful. This means that after every chapter, you need to see how you can apply that information to your life. For instance, in Chapter 5 you read about manners. There were some tips that I gave you about what you can do to show more manners. Instead of simply reading that chapter, make a plan to show better manners each day. You may make a goal to say, "yes, ma'am" and "yes, sir" at least 5 times each day.

Application means that you are doing something everyday to work on the information that you received. Each day, you must ask yourself, "Which key to success will I work on today?" You may also ask yourself, "What am I going to do today to earn this key?"

I believe in each and every one of you. I know that if you all follow these keys that I laid out for you, that you will be successful. However, if you only read this, put it on your bookshelf, and continue to do what you have always done, you probably won't be successful.

I am on this journey with you. I'm in your corner cheering you on and telling you that you can do it. Don't just have a dream, chase it. Don't just write down your goals, achieve them. Don't just want to be successful, become successful.